WHEN THE SEA SLEEPS

Poems

by

MARILYN WOOD

Child's Play

I made a bird on the smooth sand,
In the quiet time when the sea sleeps
Far out.   Choosing material from
The store at hand.   Pebbles
Worn white for the strong wings,
And fragmentary jet for the eye.
When I had finished, I stood
To admire the winging of flight
Across the rilled yellow sky,
Of the straight beating against
The sky and went away satisfied.
But the sea woke from its far off
Sleep, and crept back to the beach
Silently.   Like a truant child set
Upon mischief the prying fingers tore
The heart from my bird and cast
Its feathers, yet warm, beyond reach.
So, I came to the place again
And wept, to the mewing dirge
Of gulls.

Death of a Hare

I did not see the man
Who aimed, or hear the
Shot that bent the frightened
Grass to whisper
Death
Against the earth.
Pain, fear and one
Convulsive parabola
Were mine ...
               then silence.
Within my womb a metal
Child, its own life spent
Now spending mine, limits
My future
Counted
         in
              drops.

Death, father of life, come swiftly,
Before the heavy tread
Of man, or the soft mouth
Of the seeker, sharper than hawthorn.

No more the glorious madness
High leaping over tufts of
Knotted grass, inviting danger.

Dark roots blurred,

Faint smell of prisoned earth.
No glimpse
Of blue,
No sound
Of chasing wind......

Death, father of life,
                    come...
                              swiftly.

Here Before

I knew the flight of the bird
As it sped from the dawn end
Of the lake.
Watched its low sweep over
The waking waves, with its
Broken reflection dissolving in
Flashing points, where the water
Was light to the east.
And I knew it would turn by
The night dark reeds in the
West, in a wide loop, to fly
Back towards morning.
For I have been here before
As a watcher, in the pearl paleness
Of dawn.
So, I followed my bird with the
Eye of cyclic memory, standing alone
Beside strange waters.

Mutability of Love

"Wake up and smell the roses,"
he murmured, in the champagne
bubble moment of first love,
whispered in literal mode.
There, centre tray, mid croissants
and joy, two deep-red damask
petalled heads shed perfume,
as a blessing, on the morning
of forever.

"Wake up and smell the coffee,"
friends warned, cliched concern
covering the cracks with tea
and sympathetic ears; their
vague solutions, magazine
engendered, to cure the lost
weekends and empty bed.
"Make this", they trilled," the first
day of forever."

"Wake up and smell the future."
he hissed, in lead grey irony,
amid the wreckage of a
marriage, the bubbles burst, the
flowers faded perfumeless. He
leaves to play a part already
cast; while she, in deafening
silence, greets the first day
                  of forever.

A Haven for John Clare

(Northampton Asylum 1840)

Sensitive children took the longer route,
Through comfortable streets, avoiding
The high walls, the iron gates and
Glimpses of a life incomprehensible.
Others, with innate cruelty of youth,
Hurled current cat-calls, from the safety
Of their solid world, at isolates who
Trundled dreams across the tended grass.
A patternless dance, no music, partnerless.
Within defined parameters the lost
Found semblance of reality in wisps of
Life's long tattered fabric.
                            An erstwhile
Cleric lorded Elba, set between flower-beds,
And, gazing through the railings at the distant
Town, dreamt of a great return no less
Significant.   Hunched on a bench a
Virgin spinster wove, from others' lives, a
Husband, sons, and memories not her own,
Meticulous with names and dates conjured
By whim.

Moving among them in a
Song-filled dream, a poet carried, on his
Daily walk, a daisy-chain of words strung
By their strophe stalks, a summer pastoral
Of hawthorn brakes and nightingales, of
Leaf-fringed sunshine and the moon-glazed
Pools that childhood knew.
                    Like migrant birds,
The inmates viewed an alien world with sidelong
Glances, ready for flight on comfortable wings
Of fancy, fearful of snares set by the strong,
Who seemed to block their one desire,
Nameless and formless, so deeply felt but
Lacking spirit that might forge the padlock
Key.   And so, from dawn to dawn, they
Wandered corridors and rooms strangely familiar.
Deprived of links with earlier voices, earlier
Hopes, they shaped the passing hours into
A world more meaningful and safe.

Otters

My grandfather said
that in the clip-clop,
candlelit time of
his youth, otters lay
beneath the twisted
willow roots, and fished
the dappled moonpools
all night long.

Then factories came to
stride the water-meadows,
fish no longer danced
in sandy shoals, or
picked the stony beds
for unseen food; then
rippling patterns ceased
at dawn and dusk.

Now, in the time of
new green politics,
the water runs a
little clearer, and
intrepid fish lure
back the kingfisher
who may, in turn, call
home the dispossessed.

Spring Villanelle

In March, each morning glows anew,
With myriad colours, mirrored bright
Through glassy prisms made of dew.
Beneath each hedgerow, pushing through
The dismal wrack of winter's blight,
In March, each morning glows anew.
Wild violets with purple hue
Sparkle, when turning to the light,
Through glassy prisms made of dew.
Pale sunlit sheen of primrose, too,
Beneath the woodland's lofty height,
In March, each morning glows anew.
Retreating snow makes rendezvous
With drifts of snowdrops, dazzling white,
Through glassy prisms made of dew.
And so, in just a month or two
The land awakes to sound and sight;
In March, each morning glows anew,
Through glassy prisms made of dew.

Spider

I wished for nothing more,
Hung
    between
        nettles in the
Semi-darkness.   They left me
Alone, skirting their wilderness
With vague gestures of appreciation,
Avoiding contact with
Dark territory .... mine.
              Alone,
Poised on crystalline rods of
Fragmented light, I lived secure
Until they left.
          Unheard,
The spinney voices whispered.
          Unkempt,
The grass guarded its
Secrets.
     Then one day footsteps
Echoed again, feet unafraid of
Damp or thorn, trampled the
Places quiet so long.
          Undergrowth
torn away ....

huge blocks
of sunlight
crush cold earth;
And we,
Children of shadows, now
                        hang
blinded
        and
            dispossessed.

Vespers
(Filgrave)

White wall
        and frozen candle flame,
Plain wood
        and icon glow, create
        a stillness within sound,
        a peace transcending
            language.
Deep in the spinney pigeons treble
Soft antiphony, as shadows lengthen
        in the green,
        cool aisles.
Through open casements, a dusk-
drift
of wood smoke mingles blue with
pearl-grey incense,
stirring a sleeping memory,
or half-forgotten dream.

The Weald

Along the weald, across the wold,
A chill wind steals its way,
Then red and green, and brown and gold
Leaves fall in disarray.

Along the wold, across the sedge
A damp wind makes its way,
Bright berries glisten in the hedge
For birds that care to stay.

Along the sedge, across the mere
A rough wind makes its way,
The last brave leaves are turning here,
And soon will die away

Across the mere, across the land
A cold wind starts to blow,
Autumn retreats, as Winter's hand
Summons the ice and snow.

Twilight

The absolutes of night and day,
Of black and white, meet at
This trysting gate of subtle tones.
The animals of sun and moon
Pass in the hedgerow shade
And woodland fringe, intent
On sleep or prey.   The choirs
Of birds reduce to single choristers
Who, lacking competition, claim
A brilliance undeserved.   And,
As the pearly opalescence
Deepens, the first bright star
Heralds approaching night.

Sea chant

Here none disturb,
Save the bell tolling the dead wave
And the seawrack gently turning
Among the marbling bones.
Only the hollow shells, listening
To the song of centuries, store
That song for coming generations' ears.
Life, as a murmur through the green cloud,
Changing in degrees from emerald to milky
Jade, swiftly diffuses through the pulsing sea
And bears that lapping whisper softly on,
'Remove, replace, rebuild, regenerate'
The ancient dirge of life, and death in life,
The cycle of creation and before.
While I lie waiting to become a part
Of life.   Cresting foam flung by winds
Of time, dispersing only to rejoin and live
Again.   Continuing existence with no end
Foreseeable, in man's small grasp of time.

Passengers 1965

They sit with closed unwelcome faces. Watching
The dull landscape pass .... minutes
Of twisted trees and hours of faded hedgerows.
Unsmiling, uncommunicative. And the
Metal beat of the train drains the heart,
And adds another wrinkle to the hour-glass
Faces. Caught in their little world of travelling
Together, they remain alone. Eyeing companions
From behind turned papers in curious indifference.
They sit, carefully spaced, bending with the
Motion of the train .... But never too far. Hands
Grope for fallen books or patterns, comment
Is unnecessary. Emergency stop, and the urge
Is almost compulsive, mentally. The biro-filled
Crossword stagnates, white unanswered spaces
Mock, but who dare ask for suggestions?
Eyes rest on print, or the passing countryside;
Bodies sit impassive, but behind the closed,
Unwelcome faces minds wander at will,
And secret smiles speak freely

Snow Rondeau

Upon the night with touch serene,
Riding the breath of winter keen,
The snowflakes fall with moonlit glow
Onto the sleeping fields below.
Giving the trees a ghostly sheen,
Massing on grass, and in between
The solid furrows, where the green
Of summer bounty died, to flow
Upon the night.

....

They fall masking the corners mean,
Making dark twisted places clean;
And on the river rushes throw
A sparkling cloak, so they forgo
Their upright stance, gently to lean
Upon the night,

Haiku Year

White, shadowed by blue,
Blankets sleeping fields, only
Marked by secret paths.

Imprisoned currents
Coil in bright glass, impatient
For their destiny.

Pale fingers probe the
Icy depths of earth, and move
The dormant spirit.

Kaleidoscopic
Petals, breeze patterned, arouse
The frozen sense

Deep in the blackthorn,
Secret in lace-edged gloom, the
Cuckoo echoes now.

Coursing through veins, with
Ever quickening pace, the
Emerald blood sings.

Blue reflects blue, in
Summer's mirror-play, while bright
Foam wrinkles the sand.

Like iridescent
Gulls the butterflies skim their
Swaying yellow sea.

In fairy rings, by
Moonlight's pallid gleam, mushrooms
Bubble through dark grass

Bronze skeletons fall
To the warring breeze, seeking
Honourable graves.

Mist curling through twigs,
Wisps of trailing chiffon shroud
Symptoms of decay.

Above frost-tipped trees,
Guarding the fast dying year,
A single star

The Falcon

I saw a man who,
In the pearl-grey morning light,
Lifted his hands to
Some free spirit quartering,
Avidly, the dew fresh sky.

He whistled to the
Empty air and waited, with
Face upturned eastward.
Then called a secret name, in
Clear pitched tone, enticingly.

High, an asterisk
Marking its prey wheeled swiftly
Earthward, now checking
Its speed, to land upon an
Outstretched glove.

Lady in red

She always wore red,
Whatever time of day,
It claimed her as an acolyte
Of lust for life, or deeper desires.
In youth, poppy bright, she
Stood tall and tossed her sexuality
In the breeze, and called it living.
Later, she wore scarlet, as though
Defying those who thought her so but,
In reality, more in the wish than
The fulfilment.   She pinned her heart
On her sleeve but it was barely
Noticeable and, therefore, damaged.
Lastly, she wore crimson, when life
Had passed her by, with crushed
Petals and broken stem to mark its
Passage; a colour to hide the stain
Of her final desperation.

The Nene

A multi-coloured thread hemming
The fields, the woods, and hidden
Pools where kingfishers flash a
Trilogy of hues; where otters come
In search of bygone haunts and
Rainbow prey.   A silver thread,
Stitching the villages and thorps
Into the weft of history. Castles and
Manors, farms and ancient forts
Embroidered on the tapestry of time.
A secret thread, that drew the coracles
Of distant kin, the longships' havoc,
And cargoes of commercial greed.
A fluid pattern, broadening as it flows,
Succouring failing crops in sun-scorched
Fields; suspending movement in the
Ice-bound nights. It carries on its
Surface reflections of a modern age,
The brilliance of a high-tech world
That will be dust before the river
Fails.   And we who live within its
Rule, are bound by an invisible thread
To mystic forces chanting in its depths.

The Magpie

Proud on the lawn the magpie holds his ground
Against intruders, who would snatch his prize.
Immaculate in evening dress, profound
In thought, he looks at all with sly surmise.
At dusk he gathers with his kind in glee,
Whose chilling cackle makes their presence known
Taunting the brooding mother's misery
Of empty nests before her young have flown.
Alone, in groups, the magpie fearless goes
Marauding through the garden-scape at will,
And any other bird innately knows
That without thought or care he's primed to kill.
Yet, when he flexes both his wings in air
Those ebony and ivory fans are fair.

The Saint Nicholas Express.

Changing points ring out a carol,
Signals show the way is clear,
Usher in the Christmas special
Running only once a year.
Blowing clouds of snowy vapour,
Coach and paintwork gleaming bright,
Frequent stops for distribution,
Not a second lost tonight.
For at dawn, the run completed,
Parcels gone and whistle blown,
It's back to that well-hidden siding
Until another year has flown.

Dawn

And I have watched,
In the chill dawn,
Cold white hanging
On needle points
Of sleeping grass.
Watched the insomniac
Breeze rolling in waves through
Grey forms of tired trees.
Soul rising,
Caught in a moment of
Splendour, a moment of stillness
Inexpressible.
And, as the first pale
Yellow fingers prodded into life
All living things, there was the
Pain of loss,
The sense of a vanished peace
Incalculable.

Swedish Autumn

In the deep places
of the
forest
the kantarella group,
a blaze
of orange
in the pine-dark shade.
And, on the
moor,
the lingon glows like
scattered embers,
scorching
the bracken fronds that
kindle next
the birch and sycamore
to sudden
flame.
And burning beauty spreads
across the land,
skirting the lakes
and racing for the shore.

Two foxes

Yours,
      a surge from shadowy
grass, a whisper of autumn
leaves brushed in flight,
      a hint of gold in
        twilight.
For a brief moment fear
of surprise
        immobilised,
then beauty shattered in
sound and motion.
Later,
      from the field fringe, a
bark of defiance spanned the
moonlight, challenged
            intrusion.

Mine,
      tracking the only
path, white on a moonless
night, down the middle of
the road,
        paused
          for an
instant, low-crouched, yet
disdainfully glancing back
over humped fur. Beamed light

reflected green tinge in amber
eyes, unblinking.
     Then, unaware
of movement, the road was
empty;
     verge grass swayed
gently,
     leaving doubts
of his reality.

A Refugee Song

Brother, my brother,
Oh, do not look back,
The clouds are all ashes,
The earth is burned black.
Brother, my brother,
Just live for today,
For tomorrow exists
Many lifetimes away.

The wind in the pines
Sings a song of the free,
But it's only for others
Not you and not me.

Sister, my sister,
The evening has come,
With a cold biting wind
And no hope of a home.
Sister, my sister,
Keep looking ahead,
For the life we once knew
Is now over and dead.

The wind in the pines
Sings a song of the free,
But the music has faded
For you and for me.

So, before you all venture
Out into the fight,
Take warning of this
And remember our plight.
For a single hand raised
Though brave, will not gain,
War is pure madness,
And blood spills in vain.

And the wind in the pines
Sings a song of the free,
Today it's for others
Tomorrow we'll see,
It may be for you, and even for me.

The 'Antiques Roadshow' fan

Mrs. Brown, at number three,
Settled, with a cup of tea
To watch, with unalloyed delight
Another's treasures, yet not quite
So sanguine when a battered tray,
Just like the one she'd thrown away,
Reached some ridiculous price when sold,
'Too plain, too dark, and not so old',
Thought Mrs. Brown, yet still she sat
Through hours of other people's tatt.
One afternoon, at half-past three,
She saw the folk of Pevensey
Queuing with bags, from which stuck out
A fishing rod, a teddy's snout,
A thousand treasures, large and small,
Were hauled into the old Town Hall.
The experts murmured this or that
About a table, doll or bat,
Lauded the intricacies of treen,
When, suddenly, upon the screen
The camera focused on a pot,
In green and orange, with a lot

Of figures working here and there,
'Aunt Mildred's vase, it is I swear'
Screamed Mrs.B., then silent fell
To hear the learned expert tell
Its owner that the pot was rare,
And named a price she hardly dare
Believe. 'I saw it not so long ago',
She thought, and started rummaging below
The stairs. Amid the cobwebs, dust and rot
Were umpteen things but not the pot.
Next to the garage, where laid to rest
Were objets d'art, now past their best.
At last, a corner at the back
Revealed the pot, wrapped in a sack.
She held it high, it was the same,
'It's Tang or Ming, or some such name.'
She plucked it carefully from the rest,
And clutched it tightly to her chest.
Just as she opened the back door
She tripped, the pot fell to the floor.
The shattered pieces flew through air,
And history scattered everywhere.
Then Mrs.B. saw, as she must
Her dreams of wealth reduced to dust.

The River

Like a silken thread, stitching pages
Of history together, the river tumbles
And glides its long way home. Within
Its depths fish lie motionless, fearing
The flash of blue and bronze. By muddy
Shallows grass-laden breath ripples
The surface, before tongues reach out
For satisfaction. In secret stretches
Coot and moorhen scuttle through the
Business of the day, nests hidden
From the twilight visitors, who pad
Noiselessly in search of opportunity.
She is never silent, she folds into
Herself life in all its forms and
Times, as she wanders slowly on her
Journey. And, from the trees hunched
On the bank, the willow fingers
Strum the water's song.

The School Play.   (Alcestis)

The play has ended. Illusion blends
Into reality, and dreams dissolve
With programmes thrown away and
Exit signs. House lights reveal the fraud,
The paste, the patched, the temporary.
Behind our faded curtain a column
Holds the now deserted stage, while
Demi-gods, assuming normal roles, await
The praise of relatives and friends.
The glory that was Greece, in three
Short nights, has swiftly blossomed and
As swiftly died. While some will greet
Its ending with relief, others look back
Regretfully on what has been, and
Dread tomorrow's echoing emptiness

Aurelian Meditation 3:3

Swilling the iron estuary a
night wave, glittering with
low-hung yellow stars, shudders
the concrete shore.
          Upon the swell
               a boat
                    moves
          like a sleeper
               turning
          on a dream.
Expand, contract, as the sea breathes
cold sighs that echo fear among the
lonely passages of time.
'You embark',
                    with only a vague
idea of the destination. The
last link furrows a limpid
surface, then is drawn aboard
dripping -----
                    weeping?
'You make the voyage'.
                    The point
of departure diminishes and
becomes pointless. Do not
look back --- there is no one

to acknowledge your identity,
and the future offers only
emptiness.
The journey is all; sea-song
and seawrack the only certainties,
each wave eternity.
'You reach port'.
                  Beneath the
grape-green dawn a city rises square
against the sea.   Streets wait
and windows question blank faced.
A gangplank, fragile bridge
between then and now, spans
           the lurking terror,
           the final insensibility.
Rubbed wood against the sole.
Against the soul?
Beyond the empty quay lies
Nothing
       – or another Nineveh?
'You step ashore'.
                  Step down.
Test the validity of your
passport.
"There are gods everywhere,
           even yonder."

Village Church.

Dodging the bullet-bright sunbeams tearing
Through leaves, into the chill of centuries stored
In grey stone. No jackdaw chatter here, where
The dead communicate in other-worldly tones,
On higher planes than picnic basket spread.
Squeals of delight at crisps and chocolate bars.
While here is food for thought. The squire and
His wife rest comfortably on rock, speared by
Bright moted beams of silver gilt, while
Unforgiving pews deny a doze or cosy
Contemplation.   I shall sit in this dusky,
Dusty church until the day wears thin,
And shadows lengthen over sleeping souls.
Then I shall leave this sanctuary, returning
To the brashness of the world, bearing the
Quiet coolness for a while.

Windy Conditions.

October came, the North Wind stirred,
Deep in an icy waste,
He rubbed his eyes and stretched his legs
Preparing for the chase.
Then off he went with crafty glee,
To cause as much distress
Throughout the day, to maid and man,
And leave a dreadful mess.
He knotted blankets, tangled sheets,
Unpegged each pillow case,
And covered bushes and small trees
With items fringed with lace.
He rode a bedspread for an hour,
Then dropped it on an oak,
He danced a blouse across the fields,
Surprising simple folk.
Two towels fandangoed here and there,
It was a pretty sight,
Then, joined by socks in various hues
They filled the fading light.
Like parachutes some dainty bras
Floated through the air,

Beckoning now, with merry signs,
Some other underwear.
Throughout the day the North Wind played
With anything loosely bound,
Tossing strange objects in the air
Then littering the ground.
So, on and on the North Wind raced
Across the countryside,
Gathering playthings in his arms
Then scattering far and wide.
Creating havoc, until dusk
Spread darkness over all,
Then left his fun and turned for home,
Letting the breezes fall.

Christmas Dawn

Delicate glitter of frost on grass,
Intricate pattern of snowflakes gliding,
Prophets' promises come to pass,
Fragile flesh the godhead hiding.

Softly anthems from the skies
Tell a mystery unfolding,
Word of God in human guise,
Truth an infant form is holding.

Bless this day,
Kneel and pray
Thoxa si Kyrie.

Life and loss,
Crib and cross
Thoxa si O Theos.

The Lost Key.

On Tuesday eve, at seven or so,
The village choir meets, to go
Through anthems, hymns and music holy,
Sung at a pace, or sometimes slowly.
And oratorios, some by Bach,
Or Handel, Faure, into the dark
Go sonorous notes that upward fly
To please the ears of those on high.
The four sopranos, OAPs,
Who in the past could reach with ease
The topmost notes, now take a shot
And sometimes win, and sometimes not.
The tenors, too, are past their prime
And at high registers sometimes mime.
Basses and altos, more secure
In lower depths, feel really sure
Of carrying a tune that's true,
Where deviations are but few.
Yet, there are times when all goes wrong,
When there's no pattern to the song
From the beginning. How can this be?
The answer is, they've lost the key

That locks all singers into one
But causes chaos when it's gone.
Without it choirmasters break
And leave confusion in their wake.
All sections of the choir lose touch
With notes and pauses, drones and such
That make the pieces crystal clear,
And pleasing to the listener's ear.
Sopranos fall and basses rise,
Passing each other in surprise.
While altos pinch the tenors' part,
Try for a time and then lose heart.
Thus lively pieces turn to dirge,
And congregations have the urge
To creep back home and make some tea
To sip while watching soap TV.
On Sunday they are duty bound
To sit impassive at the sound,
But concert ticket sales will fall
When discord reigns. And so to all,
The watchword of each choir should be
"We'll never, ever lose the key."

Reflection

In winter,
        to think of
Petal bloom and green bud
Days with pleasure
        not sadness.
To hold, hand-cupped, one
Summer butterfly, and not
Disturb the
        vital dust.
To feel a warm breeze
Smile, and never envy
As it rides the grassy
Waves, its birthright
        liberty.
This is to drink the
Essence of the year and
Warm the heart

        in winter.

Interlude.

In a field
bounded by pylons and the
railway line, by threads of
power and sound,
a boy stands
in a web of silence,
fragile as winter sun.
A blur of passengers,
swaying north to Nottingham,
see him, amber caught,
and envy, for diverse reasons,
a boy in a field
bounded by youth and imagination.

"When I catch him I'll kill him
I will. I won't cry, not I, I'll
hit him till blood runs dark from
his nose, I'll close his eyes. I'll teach
him who's strong, he's wrong if he thinks
I care, that I'll cry.
I may stand here forever and die,
then he'll be sorry.
Perhaps I can find my way home

and play in the streets,
that beats this rotten old field any day.
'Hide and seek' he said hours ago, and
I've called and no one answers.
We shan't be friends any more. I'll .....

In a field
a small boy, fiercely immobile,
stands deep in feathered grass,
and travellers pounding to Preston
smile, failing to recognise
pain in the boy in a field,
bounded by loneliness and fear.

The Magi.

Three kings came riding out of the night,
They had ridden long, they had ridden far,
Following a white path over the sand
That came from the light of a burning star.
            Jaspar, Melchior, Balthazar.

Each carried a gift for an unknown child,
For an unknown God they would soon adore,
And as they covered the weary miles
Each silently thought of the gift he bore.
            Jaspar,Balthazar, Melchior.

And Jaspar smiled as he thought of a child's delight
At the sparkling, burnished gold, a kingly sight.
And Balthazar laid his hand on the incense he
brought,
While he offered his life and love to the God he
sought.
But Melchior, in the silence, breathed a sigh
For his myrrh was a sign of one who must surely
die.

Three kings rode softly in Bethlehem,
Through sleeping streets with none to see,
And at last in a stable roughly hewn
These proud men humbly bent the knee,
>   To the King of Kings,
>   To the Lord of Light,
>   To the Son of God
>   Born in poverty.

Mrs Green

Mrs Green, at number seven,
Sure that she will go to Heaven,
Lists the faults of those around her,
Letting nothing there confound her.
Last Thursday, while she dusted all,
She found an angel in the hall.
She took the matter in her stride
Thinking, with no little pride
That it was only right and meet
To put her first in all the street.
"You think you're better than the rest"
He said,"and that you should be blest.
But that's a sin and you must pay
By serving others every day."
He disappeared, she shook her head,
And disregarded what he'd said.
But now an income fall has made
Her take a job, so she is paid
To usher children, bright or fool,
Across the road towards the school.

Triolets

The writing group

On Thursday morning, close on ten,
We sit and listen, write and read.
We spill our thoughts with eager pen
On Thursday morning, dead on ten.
We cover pages fast, and then
Discover they are tales indeed.
On Thursday morning close on ten,
We sit and listen, write and read.

Midsummer

The sky is leaden, full of rain,
No day to plan an outdoor trip,
No sign the sun will shine again.
The sky is leaden, full of rain,
The droplets sing a sad refrain,
A metronomic drip on drip.
The sky is leaden, full of rain,
No day to plan an outdoor trip.

Are you sitting properly?

A solemn semi-circle sat, awash with trepidation,
The content of the next two hours was fraught with
consternation.
The lecturer, so quick and lithe, had come to give a
tweak
To the way we read our 'offerings', in fact on how
to speak.
The rustling of the paper was like dry leaves in the
breeze,
And the faint percussive knocking was the product
of our knees.
We learned to lift the sternum and locate our
'sitting bones',
And stretched and bent with gusto, suppressing all
our groans.
"Pretend you're at a funeral, and let your features
soften."
" Well done," she said. "Not really, we practise that
quite often."
And so, for half an hour, we sat and stood and
walked,
Until the moment came when, eventually, we
talked.
"Let's hear somebody read", she said, in a a voice
so bright and gay,

But, not eager for selection, we all looked the other way.
She chose her victim carefully, one cowering in her chair,
"You're a Russian from Murmansk," she cried "deliver it with flair."
The second was a pregnant Czech., the third was from Trieste,
And with accents wild and wonderful we did our level best.
We met our faults quite bravely, and glowed at words of praise,
We worked the full two hours and finished in a daze.
And what verdict did we come to, released from stress and strain?
"We really did enjoy it, we could do it all again".

Harvest

Bring to His house the bounty of His hand,
Lay at His feet the riches He has shared,
Harvests of river, sea and land,
Things flourishing at His command,
Proclaim together that the Lord has cared.

> He is the warmth of summer rain,
> He is the gentle breeze that blows,
> He is the fruit, the swelling grain,
> He is the source of everything that grows

The seed that gives you food,
The seed that gives you breath,
The seed that is renewed
And comes to life through death.

This is the Lord,
This is the Lord.

Three Gifts

They brought a rose as fair as love
To the child in a manger bed,
But he stretched his hand to feel the thorn
At the heart of the masking red.
They offered a staff as strong as life
To the child of poverty,
But he stretched his hand to feel the wood
Of a cross on Calvary.
They gave a ring as bright as joy
To the child there in the hay,
But he stretched his hand to feel the strength
Of nails on the final day.

Don't stand too close to the edge

Don't stand too close the edge dear,
A cliff is a dangerous place,
One moment you're watching the gulls dear,
The next you're with them in space.
The sea is a beautiful blue dear,
But at this time of year very cold,
You'd die in a trice if you fell dear,
So step back if you want to grow old.

Don't stand too close to the edge dear,
A sky-scraper's exceedingly tall.
Yes, people do look like ants dear,
But get larger the further you fall.
The skyline is great I agree dear,
A mixture of commerce and spire,
But one slip on a pebble up here dear,
You'd be joining the heavenly choir.

Don't stand too close to the edge dear,
There is plenty of time to board.
The platform is wet from the rain dear,
So imminent death is assured.
Can you feel the wind on your face dear,
Fierce, like a cyclone through sedge?
Oh dear, she's been sucked on the track now,
For standing too close to the edge

The Fourth Magus

There are no paths in the desert,
no signs to show the way they went,
spent is my measure,
long since,
of all but thin blood. This yellow
world frowns as the dry wind blows,
then becomes inscrutable; mutable
is hope, ambition, faith.
No signs to show the way they went,
spent is the light. For me the star
died days, weeks, centuries ago,
splintered in piercing fragments like
unshed tears.
Sand-blind with fine dust I grope,
within darkness, seamed with crimson
scars, mars my vision and understanding.
The star died long ago in a scatter of
grey ash on a lost hillside.
            Did they find what we sought?
            The seed of Zoroaster,
            The burning One, who steps
            sure-footed on disintegration,
            who heralds the river of iron
            incandescent.
I had my gift for the Lord of the
Elements ..... jewels to mirror a power
that was before is, and shall continue.

The perpetual fire flickering in the cold glow of the
ruby.
Accept.
The sky-reflecting water lapping gently in the
sapphire.
Accept.
The invisible zone of air caught pulsing in the
diamond.
Accept.
The deep power of all growth throbbing in the
emerald.
Accept.
But there are no paths, no signs to
show the way they went, spent is
my measure ... the jewels have gone
long since;
food for the hungry,
help for the sick and aged,
freedom for the slave,
until nothing remained.

The others rode on unhindered, no one
asked them for aid, no one stayed
their way star-led; no one said
"Help us. Leave your dream, look on
the faces of the poor, oppressed and
sick. We are your truth, your
ultimate reality"

Joseph was a sad man

Joseph was a sad man, a sad man was he,
The maid he chose to be his wife now caused him
misery.
Who then had seemed so chaste and mild,
Now great with child.

> But Mary said "There is no sin
> Where God himself has entered in
> To lay His son into the care
> Of a virgin pure and fair."

Joseph was a sad man,whom others seemed to
mock.
The choice of bride had made him the village
laughing stock.
"You thought her chaste, now she'd defiled
With someone's child."

> But Mary said,"There is no sin
> Where God himself has entered in,
> To lay His son into the care
> Of a virgin pure and fair."

Joseph was a sad man but then a stranger came,
A messenger new sent by God, and wrapped in
flame.
"Lift up your heart, she is still chaste and mild.
Holy the child.

> And Mary said,"There is no sin,
> Where God himself has entered in.

To lay His son into the care
Of a virgin pure and fair.
Joseph was a glad man, and a glad man was he,
"Forgive my stubborn pride and doubt, for you shall be
Forever, unto ages, chaste and mild.
Blessed your child."
And Mary said,"There was no sin,
When God himself had entered in,
To trust His only son so holy,
To this handmaiden lowly.

Easter 1

Within the earth the iron lay,
Within the forest grew the tree,
Both destined for the fatal day,
Both borne to Calvary.
Furnace forged, and roughly sawn,
Cross to hold and nails to gnaw;
Leather scourge and crown of thorn,
   Mortal pain absorbed the sorrow,
   Mortal death affirmed the morrow,
 Glory's price the Godhead bore

Easter 2

The scent of thyme and spikenard,
Herbs held in supple hands ripe
For anointing.
A pre-dawn coolness lingers on
The path that leads to expectation.
Then, as night melts, surprise
Of revelation;
      The inaccessible made easy,
      The filled now empty, and
      Death stripped of invincibility.

Pentecost.

He called their names, He touched their hearts,
They left their homes and kin,
Unquestioning they followed straight
Their service to begin.
No backward glance,
No fleeting doubt
To snare their souls in sin.

He spoke their names, He knew their hearts,
They served Him night and day,
Unquestioning they did His will
So eager to obey.
No task too hard,
No way too long
Could fill them with dismay.

He blessed their names, He held their hearts,
Though unseen from above,
Unquestioning they kept the faith,
Trust in eternal love.
With tongues of flame,
And new found strength
Descending like a dove.

The recipe

I peeped inside the glossy book,
Designed for those who cannot cook.
Within whose pages lay the cure
For pressing problems, I was sure.
A week ago a careless 'Yes'
Landed me in such a mess.
With that one word, a big mistake,
I had agreed to make a cake,
Not for our tea, oh dear me no,
But for the annual village show.
Oh, what possessed me, what cheap thrill
Caused me to lie about my skill
With flour and eggs, and milk and stuff,
When simple truth would be enough
Forever to elude the woes
Of baking cakes for local shows?
There is still time to own, confess,
Before I make the greatest mess
This yearly trial has ever seen,
Disgrace upon the village green.
But no, I'm made of sterner stuff,
A simple recipe's enough
To rescue shattered reputation
From dire, abject humiliation.
What, none of such simplicity

Quite understood by such as me?
Oh, I give up, I cannot cope
With metric measures, there's no hope
That I'll produce, within a day,
A gateau worthy of display.
No sponge as light as thistledown
Will grace my spot, or win the crown;
Which others take, as if by right,
While I am cowering out of sight.
There is no recipe on earth
Can make up for the gaping dearth
Of culinary knowledge on my part.
So, let's take courage, let's take heart,
A supermarket cake disguised
With sugar flowers, you'd be surprised,
May yet avoid deserved disgrace,
And earn a liar's winning place.

A Balkan Lament

Oh, my love was blithe and handsome
Unafraid and debonair,
    But his mouth is full of mud now,
    And the ants crawl through his hair.

There was none in town could touch him
At the meetings on the track,
    But his feet grew strangely heavy
    When the bullet broke his back.

Though he wasn't one for talking
What he said was worth a thought,
    But a piece of lead speaks louder,
    And last words are dearly bought.

He was always full of laughter,
Not one for moans or sighs,
    But the smile is growing grim now,
    And it doesn't reach his eyes.

Never think aloud

Never think aloud,
Fitting the jig-saw patterns of
Ideas into a semblance of
Clarity. It's as bad as
Writing them down on the
White sheet for all to read.
Never express your thoughts on
Anything, however innocuous.
The word catcher, word snatcher
Of opinion has his own
Rules, and they can
Condemn. Never think
Aloud, someone may be
Listening.

Haikus

1
A bright butterfly
Hovers above the water.
Thirst or reflection?

2
Sun breaks through clouds, and
Raindrops twinkle on the edge
Of leaves drinking secretly.

3
I hold a flower,
Noting its beauty fading
Even as I watch

4
The fox and I stared
At each other, and I thought
'Who is judging whom?'

A Chinese Print

Caught in the moment of fulfilment,
Thought, muscle, eye aligned forever
Immobile hunter.
Never will the prey, unseen yet closely felt
Experience death, or anguish from your weapon's
Force. No gleam of triumph light
Those narrowed eyes now fixed with purpose
In the dim beyond.   This moment is
Itself, yet all eternity.
No more will horse and hunter gallop home,
Relaxing mind and muscle in the rhythm
Of earth's compelling harmony.
Forever will the steed strain to be gone
Yet wait, the hunter aim to kill
Yet stay his hand.

Plough horses

We have worked for you. Sweated
Our lives with every heaving step.
Slow footed, sure footed indifferent to
Passing seasons. Knowing only the
Rub of wooden arms in rough
Caress, the chafing kiss of harness
Swollen by rain, or cracked by
Drying suns. 'Ships of the soil'
You have called us. Our wake
The flocks of jeering gulls who,
As winter steals across the land,
Forsake blue pastures for our fresh turned
Waves. Our helm is firm and to
The changing wind our course is still
A steady line cut in unyielding seas.
We have served you well but soon
The pain of work will pass. For
We understand the look in your eyes,
Can feel the final step, and warm life
Flowing to the soil we tread.

The Precis

What is it they want from me? As
The pale blue settles to day and
The trees sleep, windless. I could
Tell them the sun has broken behind
The elms, dark cracks interwoven. I
Could show them the black arrowed
Birds, tracing their mystic patterns from
The watchful spire, but it would be
Wasted, for they never listen. I
Must only tell them what they want
To hear, that the cold shaped words
On the page have a sense, a form.
'Direct speech', does it exist? Every
Word uttered is a lie veiling our
Thoughts, moving away from truth, yet
Reaching it ultimately, indirectly. All
This I could tell them, analyse for
Them, if they would let me. But
I am tied down to my century of
Words and brief answers. I shall
Neither fight nor join them, merely
Give up trying.

A Swedish Auction

They died. There was no fuss,
For in the country, where the seasons
Move through eternal patterns, death is
Part of the unalterable law.
The house stood empty in the time
Of bird song and falling leaves.
Then one morning, a Sunday as I
Remember, cars sped from the town
Along the dirty, untrained tracks,
Parked by quiet fences and disgorged
Their mass of quick-eyed passengers.
In the grey dawn items that
Make a home were hauled
Out to the glistening grass; and then
In the grey day they lay like flotsam
On a windswept shore. Among the
Misplaced furniture the hunters stalked
With pricing eyes, noting both woodworm
And antiquity. Books, knotted in piles
Regardless of content, lay on the chairs,
And pictures turned a blushing
Face towards the shadow of the
Solid legs. High on the steps,
Surrounded by the crowd, like some
Old senator, a red faced man
Began his task of fostering out

The orphans of the house. Like
Notes in an antiphonal chant,
Sung by an eager mercenary choir,
The prices rose and died away.
The sky was dark before the
Final objects left the grass, before
The house was just a word
Devoid of substance or reality.
There was a noise of cars
Retreating down the lane, then
Silence, waiting patiently so long,
Crept back to cover what the
World had scorned to take

The Storm 1

Beaten pewter under a
storm sky the lake waits
motionless,
        the surface glassy
.... midsummer ice...
            unbroken.
Fish, pebble-bedded,
     weed anchored,
lie in mute darkness.
Piling clouds muffle bird-song,
choke the yelp of a fox soft
padding over stubble.
       Colours intensify,
tension is tangible in earth
and water.
        Suddenly white talons
            claw
        black weave ...
slow count of four....
then
     thunder
         shakes
the rooted oaks.

The Storm 2

Over dark spires
Spearing the pale twilight
I watched it flow.
Like a flood wave from
The lake it rose, rolling
Inexorably, engulfing all.
I wished it would not
Come, yet greeted it as
One always greets the
Inevitable.   The black
Horses, unbridled, unchecked,
Followed their chosen path;
Dark foam staining
The pale sky.

Coming Snow

I sensed it on my nightly walk,
And noticed in the darkened sky
The bloody pool that lapped
The edges of the moon.
And in the blackness stars,
Like flakes suspended in their course,
Burned icily, unwinking.
With every spear-sharp breath
My nostrils caught that faintly
Acrid smell of coming snow.

Winter Walk

I walked along a lost
Path between towering pines, in the
Silent season of snow, companionless.
Leaving my single track as a
Stain upon that white sheet,
As purple shadows marked
The passing day. And I was
The only thing that moved among
Those iron pillars, stretching
To the eyes' limit and beyond.
For the forest hid its life from
Strangers, and the wind slept.

Judas

Did he feel the brush
of a cheek on his lips,
as the night wind gently plucked his hair?
Did he see a forgiving
gaze in steady eyes,
as moonlight dripped on leaves in silence there?
Did he hear the tramp
of soldiers' heavy feet,
as solid branches groaned above his head?
Did he find savation's
peace awaiting him,
when he was dead?

Remembrance

Evening wine waves
Spill over pebbles.
  Bone white,
  bread white,
  unbroken.
Each draught rises in
Hypnotic loops, invitingly.
  Plunge deep.
  Drink deep of the
  bitter cup that will
  not pass.
The palate sours with blood,
And teeth crack against
Stone ....
   But you cannot reject
   the offering,
  the demanded sacrifice.
Waves congeal in thickening night,
Dark swans die in sea-song ... and
The time of hesitation is past.
  Plunge deep in the blood
  waves, till eyes swim
And ears pound the rhythm of earth
   and water.
  Plunge deep,
  sink deep in gall lees

and splintering crust.....
In the morning light the waves are
White with absolution. Gently the
Hair winds in sand, and eyes stiffen.
For the bread is eaten
                and the cup
                        drained.

Mother wouldn't like it

There's a tiger in my bedroom
Who lives beneath the floor,
Sometimes I hear him scratching
And, occasionally, a roar.
He's grabbed me by the ankle,
Or caught my little toe,
But he's got to be a secret
For Mother mustn't know.

There's a ghost lives in the chimney,
I sometimes see his foot,
As he travels up and down it
Dislodging bits of soot.
I often hear him moaning
In wind and rain and snow,
But he must remain a secret
So Mother doesn't know.

There's a body in the bathroom,
With a knife within its chest,
Unhappily it's Father,
But I think it's for the best.
He always kept on nagging,
Said, at forty, I should go,
But I'll bury him in secret
So Mother will not know.

Old Age 1

Get rid of the wrinkles, go under the knife,
Give eyes, neck and chin a brand new life.
"In my late fifties", a phrase you'd adore
To use in your seventies, or even more
To try in your eighties, but whatever you say
Remember it's hands that give you away.

Suave Dr.Fixit was clever and deft,
He cut and he pared until nothing was left
Of unsightly wrinkles, unwanted tags;
And from eyes he removed those overstuffed bags.
But whatever he did, just remember to say
It's the back of the hands that give you away.

Carlotta, the siren, determined to stay
Eternally young, whatever the way
Would keep her skin dewy, her eyes starry bright,
Although in the morning she looked quite a fright.
No one denied her, no one dared to say
"It's always your hands that will give you away".

Old Age 2

When did I lose
The ability to run for buses?
To walk quickly
Uphill, and still be able
to hold a conversation?
When did I last
Read a book and
Remember both plot
And characters for more than
Twenty-four hours?
Whose birthday can
I celebrate without referring
To my list of dates?
Old age is sinister, he shadows
For years, and when least
Expected he pounces, and
There is no way you
Can escape.

Printed in Great Britain
by Amazon

32626459R00047